THE
BOOK
OF
TRUTHS

THE BOOK OF TRUTHS

Comforting words to help us find
the truth in our lives

THE WANDERING PADDY

JAMES MOONEY

Black&White

Black&White

First published in the UK in 2024 by
Black & White Publishing Ltd
Nautical House, 104 Commercial Street, Edinburgh, EH6 6NF

A division of Bonnier Books UK
4th Floor, Victoria House, Bloomsbury Square, London, WC1B 4DA
Owned by Bonnier Books
Sveavägen 56, Stockholm, Sweden

Interior art used under license by stock.adobe.com and shutterstock.com

The publisher has made every reasonable effort to contact copyright holders of
images and other material used in this book. Any errors are inadvertent and anyone
who for any reason has not been contacted is invited to write to the publisher so
that a full acknowledgement can be made in subsequent editions of this work.

A CIP catalogue record for this book is available from the British Library.

ISBN: 9781 78530 569 6

1 3 5 7 9 10 8 6 4 2

Typeset by Envy Design Ltd
Printed and bound in Great Britain by Clays Ltd, Elcograf S.p.A.

MIX
Paper | Supporting
responsible forestry
FSC
www.fsc.org   FSC® C018072

www.blackandwhitepublishing.com

To my family and friends, who have somehow managed to tolerate my poetic ramblings and existential crises. Your patience is truly commendable.

DEAR FRIENDS AND FOLLOWERS,

I want to start by thanking each and every one of you for your support and encouragement on Instagram and TikTok. Your kind words and messages mean the world to me, and they inspire me to keep sharing my thoughts and experiences with you.

As some of you may know, I've been through some major challenges in the past few years. First, I overcame throat cancer, which was a difficult and humbling experience that made me appreciate the value of life even more. Then, like many of us, I've been struggling with the impact of Covid on my mental well-being, as well as the many changes and uncertainties that this pandemic has brought into our lives.

However, these challenges have also been a catalyst for change and growth. They've taught me to slow down, to be more present, and to appreciate the simple joys of life. They've also inspired me to start writing and sharing my thoughts on life, and to connect with others who are going through similar experiences.

In this book, *The Book of Truths*, I've written poems that capture the essence of what I've learned about life so far. I hope that they will inspire you, too, to appreciate the beauty and fragility of life, to embrace your own unique journey, and to make the most of every moment.

As the poet Linda Ellis reminds us in her famous poem "The Dash":

"For it matters not, how much we own, the cars, the house, the cash. What matters is how we live and love, and how we spend our dash."

I urge you to make the most of your dash, my friends. Let's live and love with gratitude and compassion, and let's cherish every moment we have together.

With love and gratitude,

The Wandering Paddy AKA Jamie

CONTENTS

Introduction   xiii

PART 1 – IDENTITY & BELONGING

Self   3
The Struggle   3
Things I've Learned Throughout My Life   5
Who's She   7
Six Feet Apart   12

PART 2 – LIFE & DEATH

A Father's Grief   17
Dead Babies Don't Cure Dead Babies   19
Grief Is   20
Love Me   21
I Hope That When Death Comes   23
My Dearest Dad   24
Mother   25
Shane McCarthy   26
The Lament   28
17 Summers   29
I Look Different Since Dad Died   31
The House of Mourning   32
The Smallest Coffins   33
The Pieces That Remain   34
Things I Dream   36
Getting Old   39
My Heart Lives Outside of My Body   40

Why Did Heaven Call Your Name Dad   41
My Mother's Voice   42
You Are More   43
You Left This World as the Sun Rose   44

PART 3 – LOGOPHILE

#Empathy & Poetry   50
#Grief   52
#Happiness & Joy   54
#Hate & Disdain   57
#Life & Death   59
#Life & the Fear of Dying   61
#Memory of Love   64
#Overthinker   65
#Resilience & Hope   66
#Serendipity & Life   67
#Grief Part II   70
#What if . . .   72

PART 4 – LOVE & RELATIONSHIPS

A Simple String of Words   77
Summers Past   80
But I Loved You First   82
Caoimhe   85
Few Pains Run as Deep   87
The Sad   91
The Love I Couldn't Be   92
You Made Me a Poet   94
I Crave   96
My Questionable Lies   99
Battle Buddy   101
Soulmate   102
Falling in Love With a Soul That Resonates   104
The Moon Will Keep Us From Falling Apart   106

My Daughter   108
Indelible Marks   110
I Have Found Myself   112
The Glow of the Moon and Stars   114
The Same Hand That Holds Your Hand   116
Versions of Love   118
In My Dreams   122
To My Children   124
You Are My   126
Love Me as I Am   128
And Damn, You Were Perfect   132
Some Days   134

PART 5 – NATURE & SPIRITUALITY

Sometimes the Stars Make Me Cry and
I Don't Know Why . . .   140
The Dreamers   143
When the Day is Truly Done   144
I Was a Lost Child Too   146

PART 6 – RESILIENCE & HOPE

Hope Flickers Patiently   152
I'm OK   155
I Have Cried All My Tears   156
Pillows Stained With Tears   160
A Life Without Dreams   164
The Words We Crave   166
You Are Not Alone   168

Author's Note   171
Acknowledgements   172
About the Author   176

the words herein
are those of a man
that has lived
has loved
has lost
has felt pain
has felt empathy
has felt happiness and euphoria.
has *Lived*.
　　　—Jamie

INTRODUCTION

A BRIEF OVERVIEW OF
IRISH POETIC STYLE

Irish poetry is a rich and diverse tradition that spans centuries and languages. It reflects the history, culture, and identity of the Irish people, as well as their imagination, creativity, and spirituality. Irish poetry can be written in Irish, English, Scottish Gaelic, or Hiberno-Latin, and can adopt various forms, genres, and themes. Some of the most influential Irish poets include W. B. Yeats, Seamus Heaney, Patrick Kavanagh, Eavan Boland, Nuala Ní Dhomhnaill, and Paul Muldoon.

One of the distinctive features of Irish poetry is its oral and musical quality. Irish poetry is meant to be heard and performed, not just read and analysed. The sound, rhythm and rhyme of the words are as important as their meaning and imagery. Irish poetry often uses alliteration, assonance, consonance, and internal rhyme to create a pleasing and memorable sound pattern. Irish poetry also draws on the rich heritage of Irish music, such as folk songs, ballads, laments, and airs, to create a lyrical and emotional tone.

Another characteristic of Irish poetry is its connection to the land and nature. Irish poetry often celebrates the beauty and mystery of the Irish landscape, from the mountains and lakes to the fields and forests. Irish poetry also explores the relationship between humans and nature, and the impact of colonisation, industrialisation, and urbanisation on the environment. Irish poetry also incorporates elements of Irish mythology and folklore, such as the legends of the Tuatha Dé Danann, the Fianna, and the Ulster Cycle, as well as the stories of fairies, leprechauns, and other supernatural beings.

A third aspect of Irish poetry is its engagement with history and politics. Irish poetry reflects the struggles and achievements of the Irish people, from the ancient times to the modern era. Irish poetry addresses the issues of identity, language, religion, culture, and sovereignty and the conflicts and collaborations between Ireland and other nations, especially Britain. Irish poetry also expresses the hopes and fears, the joys and sorrows, the love and anger, and the pride and shame of the Irish people.

One of the most important figures in the Irish poetic tradition is the seanchaí, or the storyteller. The seanchaí is a bearer of old lore, who preserves and passes on the oral history and literature of Ireland. The seanchaí is a skilled and respected performer, who can captivate and entertain an audience with his or her stories, poems, and songs. The seanchaí is also a teacher and a guide, who can impart wisdom and insight through his or her stories, poems, and songs. The seanchaí is a link between the past and the present, and between the people and the poetry of Ireland.

Please don't mistake all this poetry for longing, for it is the language of my soul dancing with words. Maybe I'm sharing what I need to hear, to remind myself of strength and resilience. Or maybe I'm sharing what you need to hear, to offer solace and inspiration.

Poetry often transcends the boundaries of self, reaching out to touch our hearts and in some cases, our pain and grief.

So let my verses resonate within, for they carry whispers of hope and understanding.

1

IDENTITY & BELONGING

Self

I am what I am. I can be no less . . .
>   *No more . . .*
>   *I am me . . .*
And that honestly,
Has taken me a long time to see.

The Struggle

To lay in the dark and wonder about the light,
>   *A meander to the side of life*
>   *and its denial to allow me to see more.*

I won't live my life afraid to make mistakes
They are the lessons that I need to learn
they are the chances that I need to take
they are the bridges that I need to burn

I won't live my life afraid to make a mistake.

#deepthoughts

Things I've Learned Throughout My Life

Things I've learned throughout my life.

Everything happens for a reason.
You'll realise why you went through what you did.
Sometimes you have to make decisions that break your heart, but heal your soul.
You can't change somebody who sees no wrong in their actions.
Hurt people, hurt people . . . heal and grow from trauma.
Losing a toxic person is always a win, no matter what.
Some people come into your life just to teach you a lesson, and then leave.

That's OK.

It's all part of the never-ending ebb and flow of life.

What if you simply devoted this year
to loving yourself more?

#deepthoughts

Who's She

Part I

Who's she, nobody important
Just a shadow in the crowd
She doesn't have a voice or a choice
She's not allowed to be loud

Who's she, nobody important
Just a placeholder in his heart
She doesn't have a name or a claim
She's not a part of his art

Who's she, nobody important
Just a burden on his mind
She doesn't have a dream or a scheme
She's not the one he'll find

Who's she, nobody important
Just a stranger in his life
She doesn't have a role or a goal
She's not his lover or his wife

She's nobody important.

Part II

Who's she, nobody important
That's what she used to think
She didn't have a voice or a choice
She was always on the brink

Who's she, nobody important
That's what he made her feel
She didn't have a name or a claim
She was nothing but a deal

But who's she, somebody important
That's what she learned to see
She had a voice and a choice
She was free to be

But who's she, somebody important
That's what he failed to know
She had a name and a claim
She was more than a show

Who's she, somebody important
That's what she is today
She has a dream and a scheme
She is on her way

Who's she, somebody important
That's what he'll regret
She has a role and a goal
She is someone he can't forget

She is somebody important.

Part III

But who's she, somebody important
That's what he realised too late
He wanted to give her a voice and a choice
He wanted to change their fate

Who's she, somebody important
That's what he wants to tell her now
He wants to say he's sorry and he loves her
He wants to make her a vow

But who's she, somebody important
That's what she already knows
She doesn't need his sorry or his love
She doesn't need his woes

Who's she, somebody important
That's what she feels inside
She feels proud and strong and happy
She feels alive and dignified

I am someone important.

~~Why am I alone . . .~~

You're not alone, even if you think you are.
You have some people who love you,
some who remember you,
some who hope for you.
&
– That's all you need.

#deepthoughts

Six Feet Apart

Six feet, the measure of space and time,
        Six feet –
                dividing two hearts.
       Apart
Six feet of earth,
      Six feet of air,
           Six feet of despair,
Six feet . . .
    72 inches
        182.88 centimetres
    Of
       . . .
      Grief
a scale that weighs the soul in ounces of tears and
pounds of longing. It's 72 inches of yearning
    182.88 centimetres . . .
the distance between two outstretched hands that cannot
    touch,
      the space where words hang suspended,
heavier than air.

it's the length of a shadow that stretches across our lives
      when the sun sets too soon.
    Six feet . . . the measurement of
      Grief
      . . .
        . . .

I'll never forget the terrible scars of my trauma, but the scars mean more than just pain – they signify that I lived, I survived, and I continue to thrive despite the darkness that once tried to consume me.

#deepthoughts

2
life & death

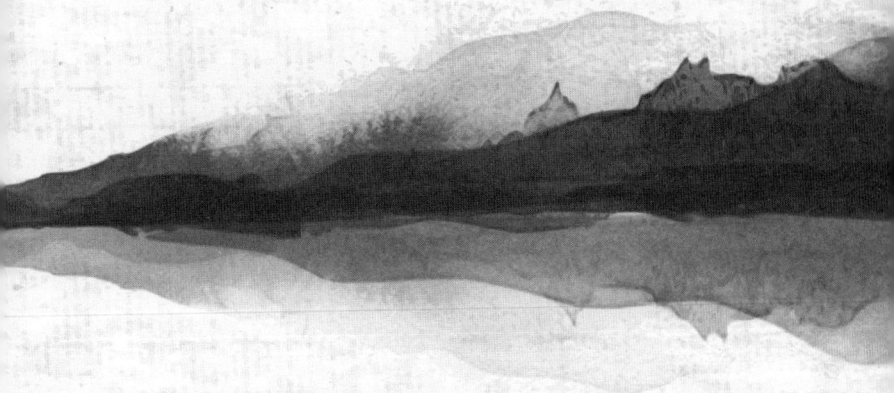

A Father's Grief

I never got to hold you in my arms
Or see your face or hear your voice
But I loved you from the moment I knew you existed
You were my child, my hope, my joy

I wanted to protect you from any harm
And give you everything you need and more
But I couldn't save you from the cruel twist of fate
That took you away before you were born

I feel so helpless and alone
As I watch your mother suffer and cry
I try to be strong and supportive for her
But inside I'm broken and I don't know why

I wonder what you would have been like
If you had a chance to live and grow
Would you have your mother's eyes or my smile?
Would you have liked music or sports or books?

I miss you every day and every night
And I wish I could tell you how much I care
But I know you are in a better place now
And one day I'll see you there

You are still my child, my hope, my joy
And I'll always love you with all my heart
You are a part of me, and *we'll never be apart*.

Why is all good poetry drenched in pain . . .
What if I was to find happiness . . .
Do I risk never been able to write
from that heart again?

#deepthoughts

Dead Babies Don't Cure
Dead Babies

Amidst the chaos, the cries of mothers' wails,
As innocence is lost, and human kindness fails,
Innocent babes, the purest of the pure,
Caught in the crossfire . . . just collateral damage I'm sure.

The ultimate crime, in the theatre of despair,
I'm losing faith in humanity it's more than I can bear,
For what madness leads to the death of the young,
Innocent lives extinguished with tanks, bombs and guns.
Our hearts heavy with grief as we watch them die.
We must remember this truth, let our voices cry.

"Dead babies don't cure dead babies"

Surely, this truth you cannot deny.

Grief Is

grief is a wave
  that crashes over me
   sometimes gentle
    sometimes violent
     sometimes calm
      sometimes stormy
      grief is a wave
       that I ride
        with my breath
        with my tears
         with my strength

    grief is a wave
that I survive

Love Me

I choose to love you in a way that speaks without
     saying anything at all.
Loving you from a distance,
in silence,
in loneliness,
and in my dreams.

But I hope one day you'll hear my voice
and feel my touch
and see my smile
and know my heart.

I hope one day you'll choose to love me back
in a way that speaks louder than words
Loving me up close,
         in harmony,
                  in happiness,
                           and in reality.

Let this one sink in . . .
There's someone out there who will
give you more in two months than you've
gotten with someone in five years.
Time means nothing.
Connection is everything.

#deepthoughts

I Hope That When
Death Comes

I hope that when death comes, it embraces us gently, like being carried to your bedroom as a child after falling asleep on the couch during a lively family party.

And in that transition,

I hope we can still sense the echoes of laughter resonating from the next room, reminding us of the love and joy that filled our journey.

And as the voices of the ones that are, fade.

The voices of those who once were, now echo in your ears.

And in that moment, the hand of the soul you miss most, will reach for you . . .

& whisper . . .

You're home.

You are home . . .

My Dearest Dad

In my heart there is an ache, that never seems to go away
For every passing day I miss the love and warmth my
father gave
He was my rock, my guiding light, my mentor and my
friend
And now that he's gone from sight, my heartache never
ends
I miss his hugs, his gentle voice and the way he always
knew
Just what to say to make me smile and chase away the
blue
I missed the way he cheered me on through every
challenge I faced and how he always had my back, no
matter what the case
I missed the sound of his laughter, and the twinkle in his
eye
His unwavering support and love, that money, just can't
buy
But though he's gone, his memory lives, forever in my
heart
And every time I close my eyes, we're never far apart
So here's to you, my dearest dad. I miss you more each
day.
And though I can't hold you close, your love is here to
stay.

Mother

In shadows deep, where memories sprawl,
I glimpse a truth, a tale to recall.
"And I see, yes I see, she's six feet under me,
But sometimes, I hope she's down the hall."

An earthy embrace, where sorrows rest,
A mother's journey, life's final quest.
Yet in the corridors of time's soft call,
I yearn for echoes from down the hall.

Now buried deep, where tears may fall,
Yet sometimes, I sense her down the hall.

A spectral hope, a whispered plea,
That in the quiet, she walks with me.
Through the rooms full of memory, where shadows sprawl,
I long to find her, down by the hall.

But in quiet moments when night is near,
I close my eyes, and hope she'll appear.
A smiling face, a silent sprawl,
And see her spirit dancing down the hall.

So, as the tears of longing flow,
In the silent spaces, where memories grow.
For in the whispers of a mother's call,
    I hope to find her waiting

        . . . down by the hall.

Shane McCarthy

In the depths of my heart lies a void so vast.
My soulmate, best friend.
Lost to demons, strife.
Battles fought their weight unsurpassed.
Leaving memories as remnants of a cherished past.
Laughter once shared, bright moments in our stride.

Our Spirits entwined, a flame that burned so bright.
Through highs and lows we faced the world's tide.
Now I'm left alone, engulfed in sorrows blight.
The demons whispered, their cruelty unbound.
They claimed your spirit a tragedy untold.

Now I wonder lost, with no solace found
in a realm of darkness where hope feels so cold.
Yet, your presence lingers, your spirits eternal flame.
In the echoes of laughter, our brightest memories were made.

And within my soul, your love remains the same
Guiding me forward thought our paths have frayed.
This struggle shapes me and gives strength to endure.
Embracing joy at the ache we once knew.
For you, my soul mate. Forever pure.
I'll carry your essence. Honouring the bond we drew . . .

*Dedicated to the memory of Shane McCarthy who lost
his battle with mental health November 30th 2022.
Requested by his wife Carol.*

Life is full of harsh lessons. Focus on the
important people in your life and not
the important things.
My harshest lesson yet in life, is that
"Graveyards are full of irreplaceable people".
Now let that one sink in . . .

#deepthoughts

The Lament

Looking back at old photographs, memories covered in dust, waiting patiently to be uncovered and cherished once more. In layers of faded colours and nostalgic hues, lies a trove of emotions and stories.
Some forgotten.
With a gentle hand, I brush off the dust, and reveal the fragments of my past that still hold meaning and power. Each photograph becomes a portal, transporting me to moments that shaped my identity, my heart. These time-worn treasures, within their delicate frames, interwoven with joy, love, grief and the echoes of my journey. Revisiting forgotten memories . . .

The dance between past and present

And thoughts of, what was, what could have . . .

And what never was . . .

"The lament."

17 Summers

Sitting over the things we bought over 17 summers together,
Baby toys, clothes and knick knacks . . . silly bits and memories
Sitting in a home without life, love and your soul.
A silence that is beyond comprehension.

To live is to love, they say . . .
Or is it, to love is to live?

A cold dark shadow rests in our love seat.
And I find myself nestled in the place, we once knew well.
Unpacking memories, next to the shadow.
Clock . . . tick tock, tick tockin in the background replaces your laughter.

Your glass sits next to mine . . . empty.
No 3am, gleeful dance . . . in the kitchen tonight.
No sunrise, no warm embrace, with your hand in mine.

Sitting over things we bought over 17 summers together.
      Grief . . . I see you now, I know your name.

Know this . . .
"You deserve the love you keep
trying to give everyone else . . ."
Now let that one sink in.

#deepthoughts

I Look Different Since
Dad Died

Someone told me I look different since Dad died
And I wonder what they meant by that
Did they see the sadness in my eyes
Or the emptiness of my heart

Someone told me I look different since Dad died
And I wish they could see beyond that . . .

Someone told me,
I look different since Dad died
And I can't get over that.

The House of Mourning

The house is silent, the clocks are stopped The mirrors
are covered, The windows are draped The spirit has left,
The window is open The family is grieving, and **black** is
their token

No music, no dancing, no laughter, no joy. No radios, no
televisions, no social events. A year of mourning, a year
of respect. A year of remembering, a year of regret

The women are in **black**, the men with **black** ties The
black diamond on the sleeve, the sorrow in their eyes
They gather around the coffin, they pray they drink they
cry They say their last goodbye, they bid their final sigh

The house of mourning, The house of pain, The house
    of love . . .
        The house of memories, The house of loss,
           The house of life,
                The house of mourning.

The Smallest Coffins

"The smallest coffins are the heaviest, they bear not just the weight of precious innocence lost, but the collective sorrow of a world that grieves the unfulfilled potential, and the dreams that will forever remain in the hushed lullabies never sung."

And on my lap
I hold her casket small and light
To her coffin
I whisper
my last goodnight

The Pieces That Remain

The worst part about losing someone you love
Is that you really don't lose them.
The memories.
The love you have for them.
The sound of their laughter ingrained in your heart.
The worst part about losing someone
Isn't the losing.
It's the pieces.
That remain.

You left me in the dark and took
the light with you.

#deepthoughts

Things I Dream

Things I dream of in a world less perfect without you in it

The first time I saw your smile, and felt my heart skip a beat
The way you held my hand, and made me feel complete
The countless nights we spent, talking under the stars
The sweet kisses we shared, and the gentle scars

The day you said yes, and became my wife
The joy of our children, and the meaning of life
The adventures we had, and the places we saw
The challenges we faced, and the lessons we learned

The moments we cherished, and the memories we made
The love we gave, and the love we received
The vows we kept, and the promises we honoured
The faith we had, and the hope we shared

The day you left me, and took a part of me with you
The pain I felt, and the tears I shed
The loneliness I endured, and the emptiness I faced
The longing I had, and the dreams I chased

Things I dream of in a world less perfect without you in it
The sound of your voice, and the touch of your skin
The warmth of your embrace, and the light of your eyes
The beauty of your soul, and the grace of your spirit

Things I dream of in a world less perfect without you in it
The day we meet again, and the eternity we spend
The peace we find, and the happiness we feel
The love we have,
     and *the love we are*

You slipped into my heart . . .
Left me speechless
Breathless
Happily, ever after . . .

#deepthoughts

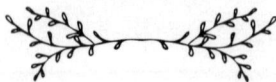

Getting Old

Tying shoelaces and getting old
Creaky knees and old regrets
People lost, people found
Understanding
Rejecting
Accepting

>   Life's ups and downs
>   smiles and frowns
>   Tis cool to use pronouns
>   Feeling out of sorts

Outdated
Past the sell by date
Peers lost, peers gone . . .

>   . . .
>   Getting old . . .
>   Where have the years gone?

My Heart Lives Outside
of My Body

When I hold you in my arms
My heart lives outside of my body
It beats in sync with your tiny breaths
And fills with love that knows no bounds

You are the miracle of my life
The gift I thought I'd never receive
You are the beautiful answer to my prayers
The dream I never dared to believe

You are the light of my eyes
The warmth of my hearth
You are the joy of my days
The purpose of my soul

You are my baby, my precious little one
My everything and so much more . . .

When I hold you in my arms
My heart lives outside of my body

Why Did Heaven Call Your Name Dad

Why did heaven call your name Dad . . . when I needed you
more than the air I breathe?

I feel the universe resonate with my heartache, a symphony
woven from the threads of grief and the unanswered
'whys'.

Why was it you?

And as I begin to navigate this world without you, I'll carry
your love within me.

And though you're gone from sight, you'll live on in the
whispers of the wind and the warmth of the sun's
embrace.

And in moments of quiet reflection,
I can still feel your presence.

So until we meet again beyond the stars,
your laughter and hugs will remain
etched in my soul,

A forever reminder of a father's love that will never fade . . .

My Mother's Voice

With just a word, a sound, a gentle tone. My mother's
voice can stir my memories.
A flood of recollection all my own. Brings back the days
of joy and reveries.
But in those moments, there's also pain. The heartaches
and struggles that we faced.
The times that we fought, the tears that fell like rain.
And all the moments that we can't replace.
And yet amidst the pain, there is still love, a bond that
nothing else can ever break,
A Love that's strong and constant, like a dove, that flies
above the chaos and the ache.
So when I hear my mother's voice again,
I'm grateful
for the love
that still remains.

You Are More

You are more than a heartbreak.
You're more than broken pieces.
You're more than the tears on your pillow.
You are more than the scars on your wrist.
You're more than the lump in your throat, the lightning
pitter patter in your chest.
You're more than the hole that was left, when they left you.

    You are more,
        so much more,
    than a little poem,
        could ever express.

You Left This World as
the Sun Rose

You left this world as the sun rose, in the light of a new day

But in my heart you still remain, in every word I say

You taught me how to love and laugh, to be strong and kind
and brave

You gave me all the best of you, and all the memories I crave

You were my mother and my friend, my guide and my support

You were the one who understood me, who always had
my back

You were the light that shone so bright, the star that never
dimmed

You were the angel in my life, the blessing that I had

You left this world as the sun rose, but you never really
left me

You live on in my soul and in my mind, in everything I see

You are the reason I am who I am, the person I aspire to be

You are the mother I will always love, the memory I will
always keep

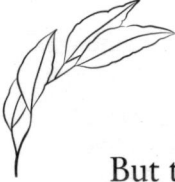

But the heart holds its own memory,
engraving every moment deep within.
I have forgotten nothing, for the heart keeps
its sacred archive of love, joy,
and even the gentlest touch of sorrow.
Every experience, every connection,
is imprinted upon its chambers, woven into
the very essence of who I am.
So, as I journey through life's intricate web,
I carry within me the vivid remembrance of
all that has shaped me.

#deepthoughts

3

LOGOPHILE

Writing poetry is a journey through a kaleidoscope of emotions. As a poet, one traverses the vast landscape of human feelings, each stanza a brushstroke on the canvas of the heart. At times, inspiration flows like a gentle stream, and the words dance effortlessly across the page – **joy** and **euphoria**. Other moments I found myself grappling with shadows – the **anguish** of unrequited love, the **ache** of loss, or the **haunting** echoes of memories. In crafting verses, we become alchemists, in the hopes of transmuting raw emotion into lyrical gold. The pen becomes a conduit for **passion, melancholy, hope,** and **despair**. And amidst it all, we discover our own humanity, etching our souls onto parchment, one syllable at a time.

Over the years I found an interest in the older forms or descriptions of these emotions, so I turned to the ancient Greek and Latin descriptions for inspiration. Even dare I say it, dipping into ye olde English (It's an Irish thing).

The following pages are a meander through that adventure. Hopefully it'll give a little insight into the language used and the re-occurring words, themes and phrases.

#EMPATHY & POETRY

Empathy is the ability to feel what another person is feeling, to see the world through their eyes, to share their joys and sorrows. It is a rare and precious gift, one that can bridge the gaps between us and make us more human. But empathy can also be a burden, a source of pain and confusion, a reminder of how fragile and vulnerable we are. How do we cope with the weight of empathy, the responsibility of caring for another soul? How do we express the depth and richness of our empathy, the beauty and the tragedy of it?

One way is through poetry. Poetry is the art of using words to capture the essence of an emotion, to create a resonance that transcends the ordinary. Poetry is the language of empathy, the voice of the heart, the music of the soul. Poetry can help us understand ourselves and others better, to heal and to grow, to celebrate and to mourn. Poetry can inspire us to be more empathetic, to reach out and connect, to offer comfort and support, to honour and to cherish. Poetry can also help us cope with the challenges of empathy, to release and to transform, to question and to learn, to forgive and to accept. Poetry can be a form of therapy, a way of coping with the bite of grief and the scar of healing, the pain and the peace, the lesson and the love of the soul.

#logophile

Poetry: the empathy of words, the resonance of emotions, the therapy of the soul.

Empathy: the poetry of life, the connection of hearts, the compassion of the mind.

"the art and the gift of the soul,
the resonance and the connection of the heart,
the therapy and the compassion of the mind."

#GRIEF

Have you ever felt like you are stuck in a loop of sadness, unable to move on from the loss of someone or something you loved? The one who left a hole in your heart, your life, your world. The one who took a part of you with them, leaving you incomplete, broken, empty. The one who you still miss, still remember, still love.

This is the feeling of **luctus** – the pain of grief. The one that weighs you down, and holds you back, and tears you apart. The one that makes you cry, and scream, and curse. The one that makes you numb, and silent, and hopeless.

Luctus is the enemy of healing, of acceptance, of peace. It is the enemy of joy, of hope, of love. It is the enemy of life. Luctus is the prison of the heart, the trap of the soul, the hell of the self.

#logophile

Luctus: the loop of sadness, the hole of loss, the enemy of life.

Sanatio: the break of sadness, the fill of loss, the friend of life.

Liberatio: the end of sadness, the closure of loss, the freedom of life.

Amor: the cure of sadness, the bridge of loss, the ally of life.

"The art of grieving,
        but also the trap of suffering."

"Luctus, Sanatio, Liberatio, Amor: the stages
of grief and healing,
        the journey of the heart and soul,
            the transformation of pain and love."

#HAPPINESS & JOY

Happiness and joy are two of the most sought-after and elusive emotions in human existence. We all want to be happy and joyful, to feel fulfilled and content, to experience the beauty and wonder of life. But what do happiness and joy really mean? How do we define them, measure them, achieve them?

Perhaps happiness is a state of mind, a subjective evaluation of our circumstances, a comparison of our expectations and reality. Happiness can be influenced by many factors, such as our genes, our environment, our relationships, our goals, our values, our beliefs. Happiness can be fleeting or lasting, depending on how we perceive and interpret our situation. Happiness can be enhanced by gratitude, optimism, kindness, generosity, mindfulness, and other positive practices. Happiness can be diminished by stress, anxiety, fear, anger, sadness, and other negative emotions. Happiness can be a choice, a habit, a skill, a challenge.

Perhaps joy is a feeling of the heart, a transcendent emotion that arises from within, a connection to something greater than ourselves. Joy can be triggered by many sources, such as nature, art, music, spirituality, love, laughter, and other forms of expression. Joy can be spontaneous or cultivated, depending on how we open ourselves to the possibility of awe and wonder. Joy can be amplified by sharing, celebrating, appreciating, and savouring the moments that touch our soul. Joy can be dampened by cynicism, boredom, apathy, and other forms of disconnection. Joy can be a gift, a surprise, a blessing, a mystery.

Happiness and joy are not mutually exclusive, nor are they interchangeable. They can coexist, complement, or contrast each other, depending on the context and the perspective. They can both enrich our lives, or they can both elude us, depending on the conditions and the attitude. They can both be pursued, or they can both be discovered, depending on the journey and the destination.

What happens when happiness and joy are missing from our lives? What are the consequences of living without them? How do we cope with the absence of these vital emotions?

Perhaps the lack of happiness and joy leads to a state of **dolor** – the pain of emptiness. The one that drains us of energy, motivation, and purpose. The one that makes us feel dissatisfied, restless, and hopeless. The one that makes us question our worth, our meaning, our direction.

Dolor is the enemy of fulfilment, of growth, of creativity. It is the enemy of passion, of enthusiasm, of inspiration. It is the enemy of life. Dolor is the void of the mind, the numbness of the heart, the darkness of the soul.

#logophile

Happiness and Joy: the meaning and the mystery of life, the mind and the heart, the choice and the gift.

Dolor and Sanatio: the emptiness and the fullness of life, the void and the fill, the enemy and the friend.

Liberatio and Amor: the freedom and the connection of life, the end and the bridge, the blessing and the ally.

Gratia and Mirus: the gratitude and the wonder of life, the enhancement and the trigger, the practice and the surprise.

"The eight emotions of life, the mind and the heart, the choice and the gift, the emptiness and the fullness, the void and the fill, the enemy and the friend, the freedom and the connection, the end and the bridge, the blessing and the ally, the gratitude and the wonder, the enhancement and the trigger, the practice and the surprise."

Happiness & Joy . . .
     & Dolor . . . Life?

#HATE & DISDAIN

If you've ever felt like you're consumed by a fire of anger, unable to forgive or forget the wrongs done by someone or something you despise? The one who hurt you, betrayed you, humiliated you. The one who took away your dignity, your happiness, your freedom. The one who you still resent, still blame, still hate.

This is the feeling of **odium** – the poison of hate. The one that burns you from within, and spreads to others, and destroys everything. The one that makes you bitter, and cruel, and violent. The one that makes you lash out, and seek revenge, and cause pain.

Odium is the enemy of healing, of understanding, of peace.

It is the enemy of compassion, of forgiveness, of love. It is the enemy of life.

Odium is the prison of the heart, the trap of the soul, the hell of the self.

#logophile

Cogitare: the torment of the overthinker, the destroyer of the dreamer, the killer of the lover.

Sapere: the delight of the thinker, the creator of the dreamer, the healer of the lover.

"The fire of anger,
the poison of hate,
the prison of the self."

#LIFE & DEATH

#Life

Vivencia: the feeling of being fully alive, of experiencing every moment with intensity and awareness, of savouring the beauty and complexity of existence. The state of mind that transcends the mundane and ordinary, and embraces the wonder and mystery of life. The sense of awe and gratitude that fills your heart when you witness something extraordinary, or when you connect deeply with another being. The joy of living vivencia, and the longing for more of it.

Vivencia: the ecstasy of being, and the hunger for more.

#Death

Thanatia: the feeling of acceptance and peace that comes from facing your own mortality, of realizing that death is inevitable and natural, and that it is not something to be feared or avoided. The awareness that death is not the end, but a transition, a transformation, a new beginning. The appreciation of the preciousness and fragility of life, and the desire to live it fully and meaningfully, to leave a positive legacy, to make a difference. The wisdom of thanatia, and the courage to embrace it.

Thanatia: the serenity of letting go, and the hope of rebirth.

#Life & Death

Ephemeria: the realisation that life is fleeting and fragile, that every moment is precious and irreplaceable, that every breath could be your last. The awareness of the ephemeral nature of existence, and the desire to make the most of it, to live fully and authentically, to love deeply and passionately, to create something meaningful and lasting, to leave a positive mark on the world. The paradoxical feeling of both joy and sorrow, gratitude and grief, hope and despair, that comes from knowing that you are alive, but not for long.

Ephemeria: the art of living in the present.

Ephemeria: the beauty and pain of being mortal.

#logophile

"Life is a precious gift that we must cherish in the present, while being aware of the beauty and pain that comes with our mortality."

#LIFE & THE FEAR OF DYING

Because I have loved life but I still fear death, I shall live each day as if it were my last. This is the feeling of **vivere** – the zest for living. The one that fills me with courage, passion, and purpose. The one that makes me appreciate every moment, every breath, every heartbeat. The one that makes me embrace the beauty, the wonder, the mystery of life.

But vivere is also a paradox, a challenge, a gift. How do I balance vivere, the love for the present, the fear for the future, the regret for the past? How do I cultivate vivere, the courage to face the inevitable, the passion to pursue the meaningful, the purpose to leave a legacy? How do I share vivere, the appreciation of the self, the connection with others, the contribution to the world?

Perhaps vivere is a state of being, a way of experiencing the world, a mode of expressing the self. Vivere can be influenced by many factors, such as my genes, my environment, my relationships, my goals, my values, my beliefs. Vivere can be enhanced by joy, happiness, peace, love, and other positive emotions. Vivere can be diminished by sadness, anger, fear, hate, and other negative emotions. Vivere can be a choice, a habit, a skill, a blessing.

Perhaps vivere is a feeling of the soul, a reflection of something greater than myself, a resonance with something deeper than my comprehension. Vivere can be triggered by many sources, such as nature, art, music, spirituality, love, humour, and other forms of expression.

Vivere can be spontaneous or deliberate, depending on how I create or recognize the opportunities for it. Vivere can be amplified by sharing, celebrating, appreciating, and savouring the moments that touch my soul. Vivere can be dampened by ignoring, dismissing, rejecting, and forgetting the moments that enrich my soul. Vivere can be a lesson, a surprise, a mystery, a gift.

Vivere and death are not mutually exclusive, nor are they interchangeable. They can coexist, complement, or contrast each other, depending on the context and the perspective. They can both enrich my life, or they can both frighten me, depending on the meaning and the purpose I assign to them. They can both be pursued, or they can both be encountered, depending on the journey and the destination.

What happens when vivere and death meet in my life? What are the consequences of living with them? How do I cope with the certainty and the uncertainty they bring?

Perhaps the meeting of vivere and death leads to a state of **memento** – the memory of living. The one that fills me with nostalgia, gratitude, and hope. The one that makes me remember the good times, the bad times, and the lessons learned. The one that makes me honour my achievements, my failures, my growth.

Memento is the friend of vivere, of joy, of love. It is the friend of life. Memento is the legacy of the mind, the treasure of the heart, the gift of the soul.

Because I have loved life but I still fear death, I shall live each day as if it were my last. But I shall also live each day as if it were my first. For vivere, memento, and death are the cycle of life, the joy and the sorrow, the love and the loss of the soul.

#logophile

Vivere: the love and the fear of life, the soul and the legacy, the first and the last.

Memento, death: the soul's trinity of love, life, and loss.

>"To live is to love and fear,
>   to leave and remember,
>   *to begin and end*"

>*"To begin and end.*
>   & the important bits in between . . .
>   to exist in the moment
>   to truly live . . ."

#MEMORY OF LOVE

Have you ever felt like you are connected to someone in a way that transcends time, space, and logic? The one who understands you, accepts you, inspires you. The one who shares your dreams, your passions, your values. The one who you still admire, still trust, still love.

This is the feeling of **anamnesis** – the memory of love. The one that fills you with warmth, and light, and joy. The one that makes you smile, and laugh, and cry. The one that makes you grateful, and hopeful, and brave.

Anamnesis is the friend of healing, of growth, of peace. It is the friend of wisdom, of faith, of grace. It is the friend of life. Anamnesis is the gift of the heart, the treasure of the soul, the miracle of the self.

#logophile

Anamnesis: the memory of love, the friend of life, the gift of the self.

Lethe: the forgetting of pain, the enemy of growth, the curse of the self.

"Remember the love that gives you life,
          forget the pain that takes it away.
                    Anamnesis and Lethe, the balance of
                    the self."

#OVERTHINKER

Have you ever felt like your mind is your own worst enemy, the one who sabotages your every move, your every word, your every interaction? The one who makes you doubt yourself, criticize yourself, hate yourself. The one who makes you replay every mistake, every failure, every rejection. The one who makes you imagine every scenario, every outcome, every consequence.

This is the feeling of **cogitare** – the curse of overthinking. The one that keeps you awake at night, and restless during the day. The one that makes you anxious, nervous, and fearful. The one that makes you avoid people, places, and situations. The one that makes you isolate yourself, withdraw yourself, and lose yourself.

Cogitare is the enemy of action, of spontaneity, of joy. It is the enemy of confidence, of courage, of love. It is the enemy of life. Cogitare is the prison of the mind, the trap of the soul, the hell of the self.

#logophile

Cogitare: the torment of the overthinker, the destroyer of the dreamer, the killer of the lover.

Sapere: the delight of the thinker, the creator of the dreamer, the healer of the lover.

> "The art of thinking,
> but also the trap of overthinking."

#RESILIENCE & HOPE

Respera: the feeling of strength and optimism that comes from overcoming adversity, of finding new ways to cope and grow, of learning from your mistakes and failures. The awareness that you are not defined by your past, but by your present and future, and that you have the power to change and improve yourself. The confidence that you can face any challenge, and the hope that things will get better. The joy of respera, and the determination to pursue it.

#logophile

Respera: the resilience of the human spirit.

Respera: the spark that ignites your dreams.

> "Your journey is fuelled by your resilience
> and your dreams.
> Don't let anything stop you from
> pursuing them."

#SERENDIPITY & LIFE

Serendipity is the phenomenon of finding something valuable or delightful when you are not looking for it, or when you least expect it. It is the happy accident, the lucky coincidence, the pleasant surprise. It is the discovery of a new friend, a new love, a new opportunity, a new idea, a new world. It is the spark of curiosity, the thrill of exploration, the joy of creation.

But serendipity is also a paradox, a mystery, a challenge. How do we explain the occurrence of serendipity, the alignment of seemingly unrelated events, the convergence of seemingly disparate paths? Is it a result of chance, fate, design, or something else? How do we cultivate serendipity, the openness to the unexpected, the readiness to seize the moment, the willingness to embrace the unknown? How do we balance serendipity, the appreciation of the unplanned, the acceptance of the uncontrollable, the gratitude for the unearned?

Perhaps serendipity is a state of mind, a way of seeing the world, a mode of being in the world. Serendipity can be influenced by many factors, such as our attitude, our attention, our intuition, our network, our environment, our actions. Serendipity can be enhanced by curiosity, diversity, flexibility, generosity, serenity, and other positive qualities. Serendipity can be diminished by cynicism, routine, rigidity, selfishness, anxiety, and other negative traits. Serendipity can be a choice, a habit, a skill, a gift.

Perhaps serendipity is a feeling of the soul, a connection to something larger than ourselves, a glimpse of something beyond our comprehension. Serendipity can be triggered by many sources, such as nature, art, music, spirituality, love, humor, and other forms of expression. Serendipity can be spontaneous or deliberate, depending on how we create or recognise the opportunities for it. Serendipity can be amplified by sharing, celebrating, appreciating, and savoring the moments that touch our soul. Serendipity can be dampened by ignoring, dismissing, rejecting, and forgetting the moments that enrich our soul. Serendipity can be a blessing, a surprise, a lesson, a mystery.

Serendipity and randomness are not mutually exclusive, nor are they interchangeable. They can coexist, complement, or contrast each other, depending on the context and the perspective. They can both enrich our lives, or they can both confuse us, depending on the meaning and the purpose we assign to them. They can both be pursued, or they can both be encountered, depending on the journey and the destination.

What happens when serendipity and randomness collide in our lives? What are the consequences of living with them? How do we cope with the uncertainty and the possibility they bring?

Perhaps the collision of serendipity and randomness leads to a state of **sudor** – the sweat of wonder. The one that fills us with excitement, anticipation, and curiosity. The one that makes us feel alive, adventurous, and creative. The one that makes us question our assumptions, our boundaries, our potential.

Sudor is the friend of discovery, of growth, of innovation. It is the friend of passion, of enthusiasm, of inspiration. It is the friend of life. Sudor is the fire of the mind, the spark of the heart, the light of the soul.

#logophile

Serendipity: the wonder of the unexpected, the soul of the discovery, the gift of the collision.

Randomness: the challenge of the unpredictable, the mind of the experiment, the lesson of the contrast.

> "The wonder and the challenge of life,
> the unexpected and the unpredictable,
> the discovery and the experiment, the
> collision and the contrast,
> the enthusiasm and the
> *possibility*."

The *possibility* . . .

#GRIEF PART II

#*The Monster That is Grief*

Have you ever felt like you are haunted by a monster that is Grief, that lurks in the shadows, waiting for the right moment to strike, to devour, to destroy you? The one who feeds on your sorrow, your despair, your guilt. The one who robs you of your joy, your hope, your love. The one who you still fear, still avoid, still hate.

This is the feeling of **morsus** – the bite of grief. The one that wounds you deeply, and infects you slowly, and consumes you wholly. The one that makes you bleed, and ache, and suffer. The one that makes you isolate, and withdraw, and escape.

Morsus is the enemy of healing, of growth, of peace. It is the enemy of acceptance, of forgiveness, of grace. It is the enemy of life. Morsus is the monster of the heart, the beast of the soul, the horror of the self.

But morsus is not invincible, nor eternal, nor absolute. It can be faced, fought, and overcome. It can be tamed, healed, and transformed. It can be a teacher, a guide, and a friend.

Morsus is the challenge of healing, of growth, of peace. It is the challenge of acceptance, of forgiveness, of grace. It is the challenge of life. Morsus is the catalyst of the heart, the ally of the soul, the miracle of the self.

#logophile

Morsus: the bite of grief, the wound of the heart, the teacher of the soul.

Sanatio: the healing of grief, the scar of the heart, the friend of the soul.

"The cycle of grief and healing,
the pain and the peace,
the lesson and the love of the soul."

#thehealingofgrief

#WHAT IF . . .

Have you ever wondered about the people you meet by chance, the ones who cross your path for a brief moment, but never stay? The ones who smile at you on the street, or sit next to you on the bus, or bump into you at the grocery store. The ones who exchange a few words with you, or a glance, or a nod. The ones who make you feel something, even if it's just a flicker of curiosity, or interest, or attraction.

What if they were meant to be more than strangers? What if they were the ones who could have changed your life, if only you had the courage, or the time, or the opportunity to get to know them better? What if they were the ones who could have made you laugh, or cry, or think, or love? What if they were the ones who could have been your friends, or your lovers, or your soulmates?

But you will never know, because you let them go. You let them fade into the crowd, into the background, into oblivion. You let them become another face, another name, another memory. You let them become another what if, another maybe, another regret.

This is the feeling of **parakalein** – the longing for the strangers who could have been. The ones who haunt your dreams, and your fantasies, and your imagination. The ones who make you wonder about the infinite possibilities of life, and the random twists of fate. The ones who make you question what is, and what could have been.

#logophile

Parakalein: the ache of the roads not taken, the faces not kissed, the lives not lived.

Eudaimonia: the joy of the choices made, the love shared, the purpose found.

Sonder: (uncountable) (neologism) The profound feeling of realising that everyone, including strangers passing in the street, has a life as complex and as vivid as one's "own", which they are constantly living despite one's personal lack of awareness of it.

Ref a conversation with Ben (Son)

"Neo – new . . . Logism – Logos – Longer definition: The Greek word logos (traditionally meaning word, thought, principle, or speech)

In short – "New Thought"

"Life is full of choices and chances . . . endless rolls of outcomes
I often wonder, ponder . . . what could have been?"

4

LOVE &
RELATIONSHIPS

A Simple String of Words

Part I

A simple string of words Can make or break a heart Can heal or hurt a wound Can start or end a war

A simple string of words Can inspire or discourage a dream Can praise or criticise a deed Can unite or divide a team

A simple string of words Can express or conceal a thought Can reveal or hide a truth Can agree or oppose a lot

A simple string of words Can create or destroy a world Can shape or erase a reality Can bless or curse a soul

A simple string of words Can do so much or so little Can be so powerful or so weak Can be so simple or so complex

A simple string of words

Words are powerful, choose yours wisely.
        A simple string of words Can bless or curse a soul.

Part II

A simple string of words
I Love you
The words I should have said

A simple string of words
I miss you

One simple word
Regret

Part III

A simple string of words
I've moved on

   #acceptance

         #deepthoughts

I doubt that people know me.
They know the fragments of me I have
shown them, fragments of me they
have imagined in their hearts.
The simple fragments of me, the simple
parts of me to know.

#deepthoughts

Summers Past

And in days like summers past
> We ran and laughed and played
> We chased the sun and caught the breeze
> We made the most of every day

And in days like summers past
> We shared our hopes and fears
> We talked and listened and understood
> We wiped away each other's tears

And in days like summers past
> We felt so free and alive
> We loved and cared and cherished
> We thought we'd always survive

And in days like summers past
> We didn't know what was to come
> We didn't see the changes
> We didn't hear the drum

And in days like summers past
> We lost what we once had
> We grew apart and drifted
> We became so sad and mad

> > *And in days like summers past*
> > *We wonder what went wrong*
> > *We miss what we once had*
> > *We wish we could belong*

And in the end, when we are gray
and old and sitting by the fire.
All I want, is your hand in mine
And that's all that really matters.

Don't look back with sadness,
look forward with happiness, for the
past's pages are written, but the
future's yet to be.

#deepthoughts

But I Loved You First

But I loved you first
Before you knew my name
Before you saw my face
Before you felt the same

But I loved you first
When you were just a dream
When you were out of reach
When you were unaware of me

But I loved you first
And now you love me too
And now we share a life
And now I'm glad it's true

But I loved you first
And I will love you last
And I will love you always

You loved me first, but now you're gone,
*   and I'm still here, alone and wrong.*

But I loved you first
Before you broke my heart
Before you tore me apart
Before you made me start

But I loved you first
When you were all I had
When you were my only hope
When you were not so bad

But I loved you first
And now you love someone else
And now you left me alone
And now I hate myself

But I loved you first
And I will love you still
And I will love you forever
Even though you never will
No matter what the past

And just like that, the pages of our
story turned.
As we faded into the realm of
strangers once more.
But it within the remnants of what once was,
lie the echoes of our shared moments.
A whispering of a connection that will
forever linger In the depths of our hearts.

#deepthoughts

Caoimhe

Even though you're all grown up, you will always be
Daddy's little girl.
No matter where you go in life, you're still the apple of
my world. I'm proud of all your achievements, I'm happy
for your success. But I also know the challenges you face,
the struggles and the stress. I'll always be here to support
you, to listen and to care. I'm always here to hug you, to
comfort you and to share. I love you more than words
can say, I've cherished every moment of your life. You're
my precious daughter, my gift.

Daddy's Little Girl.

Do you think you deserved that love?
Let me tell you this: love doesn't operate on
the principle of deserving. It flows freely,
unconditionally, and without judgment.
So yes, you deserved that love simply
because you exist, because you are worthy
of every drop of affection that graces your
path. Embrace it, cherish it, and let it
remind you of the inherent value within
your soul.

#deepthoughts

Few Pains Run as Deep

Part I

Few pains run as deep as loving the ghost of someone
who still walks the earth.
The haunting ache of longing for a connection that no
longer exists, the bittersweet dance with memories that
cannot be rewritten.

> *The heart trapped in a perpetual state of yearning,*
> *aching, grasping at fragments of a love that fade*
> *with each passing moment.*

There is no greater torment than loving a ghost,
condemned to wander the realm
    of what could have been.
Caught in the fragile balance between . . .
                holding on and letting go

Part II

You were real, even though I'll never feel you again. I miss you every day. Each dawn brings a bittersweet reminder of what once was, and I find myself haunted by the ghost of the person you used to be. The memories we shared still resonate within me, but they now exist as fading echoes, distant and unattainable.

The pain of loving a ghost lingers, and I find myself longing for a connection that has dissipated into thin air. It's like dancing with the shadows of our past, memories etched in time, unable to be rewritten. The heart yearns for what once was, aches for what could have been, and grasps at fragments of a love that slips away with each passing moment.

Caught in the throes of this eternal struggle, I find myself torn between holding on and letting go. The heart wants to cling to the memories, the love that was once so vibrant, but the mind knows that it's time to release the pain and accept that things have changed. It's a fragile balance, and sometimes I feel trapped between two worlds.

In this realm of what could have been, I wander, endlessly searching for closure, for solace. The torment of loving a ghost is a constant companion, a weight that bears down on me. Yet, I must find the strength to move forward, to cherish the memories without being defined by them.

So, I bid farewell to the past, as difficult as it may be. I release the ghost of you and embrace the person I am becoming. I'll hold the memories dear, but I won't let them imprison my heart any longer. I'll cherish the love we had, but I'll learn to love myself even more.

You were real, even though I'll never feel you again. I miss you every day. Each dawn brings a bittersweet reminder of what once was, and I find myself haunted by the ghost of the person you used to be. The memories we shared . . .

but they now only exist as fading echoes, distant and unattainable.

You were real, and I'll forever cherish the time we had together. But now, as I face each day without you, I must learn to find happiness and fulfilment within myself. So, I'll say it once more: "I miss you every day," but from this moment on, I will strive to miss you a little less, until the day comes when the ache in my heart is finally healed.

Anger is the part of yourself that loves
you the most.
It knows when you are being mistreated,
neglected, or disrespected.
It signals that you have to take a step out of
a place that doesn't do you justice.
It makes you aware that you need to leave
a room, a job, a relationship, and old patterns
that don't work for you anymore.
Learn to listen to your anger and make it
your best friend.
Then it'll leave.

#deepthoughts

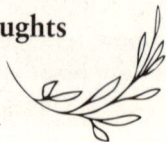

The Sad

I am not without flaws
I am imperfectly perfect.

And one day I will write about all the good things we had

. . .

And it's the *had*, that makes me sad.
    But for . . .
        But for now . . .
            I'll reminisce the sad.

The Love I Couldn't Be

I could see it in your eyes, the portals to the soul
>   The way they sparkled and shone, like stars in
>   a black hole
>   I could see it in your eyes, the depth of your
>   emotion
>   The way they changed and expressed, like waves in
>   the ocean

I could see it in your eyes, the beauty of your mind
>   The way they reflected and revealed, like mirrors
>   of a kind
>   I could see it in your eyes, the warmth of your
>   heart
>   The way they smiled and glowed, like sunbeams
>   from the start

<u>But</u> *I could also see it in your eyes*, the distance and the
>   doubt
>   The way they looked away and hid, like secrets you
>   left out
>   I could also see it in your eyes, the pain and the
>   regret
>   The way they cried and dimmed, like tears you
>   can't forget

I could see it in your eyes, the portals to the soul
        But I could never see myself, the one
        who made you whole
        I could see it in your eyes, the love you
        felt for me
        But I could never see it in mine, the
        love I couldn't be

You Made Me a Poet

In the quiet after the storm,
amidst the shards of a once-whole heart,
you made me a poet;

with every beat now a verse,
every sigh a sonnet,
and every tear . . .

a testament to a love that wrote itself into my soul,
only to erase its presence,
leaving behind shards of a once-whole heart
and the indelible ink of *memory.*

Can I go back there, back to the beginning,
where innocence was my companion
and the weight of the world had yet to find its
wayonto my shoulders?

#deepthoughts

I Crave

I crave your love like flowers crave the sun To bloom and grow and fill the air with scent But you are far away, my only one And I am left with loneliness and lament

I crave your touch like waves crave the shore To kiss and hug and mingle with the sand But you are out of reach, my evermore And I am left with longing and a bland

I crave your voice like birds crave the song To sing and soar and fill the sky with joy But you are silent, my sweet siren And I am left with silence and a ploy

I crave your love so bad it hurts my heart But you don't love me back, and that's the worst part.

I don't need you

    to complete me

I need you

    to complement me

to challenge me

    to inspire me

to support me

    to love me

for who I am

#deepthoughts

I've got to cut you out of my life,
I just can't put up with it

#deepthoughts

My Questionable Lies

I have nothing in this life but your eyes
The anchors of my heart, the bonds of my ties
The partners of my art, the mates of my lies
The lovers of my parts, the friends of my thighs

"Sure jaysus I love ya."

> "Your eyes are my everything, my heart, my art,
> my love and my questionable lies . . . "

I made a mistake,
I had hoped, you could forgive me
. . . you didn't
The end!

#deepthoughts

Battle Buddy

I sleep more and more in my dreams
Where I can find and enjoy my peace
Where I can hope and pray for a release
Where I can live and die with ease

Farewell, my friend, who lit my way with love; to die
is to rest.

A friend's note . . .
Please be more . . .

#Friend
#ILetYouDown
#I'mSorry

Soulmate

I still remember the day you left
The way you smiled and kissed me goodbye
The way you said you loved me and would always be
there
The way you promised to come back soon

But you never did

You never came back from that war
That took your life and broke my heart
You never saw our son grow up
Or held our daughter in your arms

You never knew how much I missed you
How much I cried and prayed for you
How much I wished you were here with me
Or how much I still love you

But I know you're somewhere better now
Somewhere peaceful and free of pain
Somewhere where you can watch over us
And someday we'll meet again

Until then, I'll keep you in my memory
And cherish every moment we had
Until then, I'll keep you in my heart
And hope that you're proud of me

You're still my hero, my soulmate, my everything
You're still the reason I live and breathe
You're still the one who makes me smile and laugh
You're still the one who gives me strength and hope

You're still the one I love

> *#Veterans*
> *#PTSD*
> *#22A*
> *#ReachOut*

Falling in Love With a Soul That Resonates

I'm more interested in falling in love with
a soul that resonates with mine, weaving a connection
that transcends the physical realm.
For the depth of emotions, the bonds of trust,
and the beauty of shared dreams hold far
greater allure than the fleeting pleasures
of a passing nights passion.
Love's embrace is the true ecstasy,
intertwining hearts and igniting a flame.
I'm more interested in falling into someone's heart, than
falling into someone's bed.

Love is just a decision . . .
The choice is yours

#deepthoughts

The Moon Will Keep Us From Falling Apart

The moon is our witness tonight
As we gaze at the same silver light
And though we are miles apart in space
We share a bond that time and distance cannot erase.

Sometimes I lie awake and I think of you
And wonder if you miss me too.
I wish I could hold you in my arms
And feel your breath and your loving lady charms.

But I know that soon, we will meet again
And our love will overcome the pain
Until then my sweetheart, I'll keep you in my heart
    And the moon will keep us from falling apart.

    #underthesamesky

love is not easy
it takes work
it takes patience
it takes compromise
it takes sacrifice
it takes courage
it takes love –
to love.

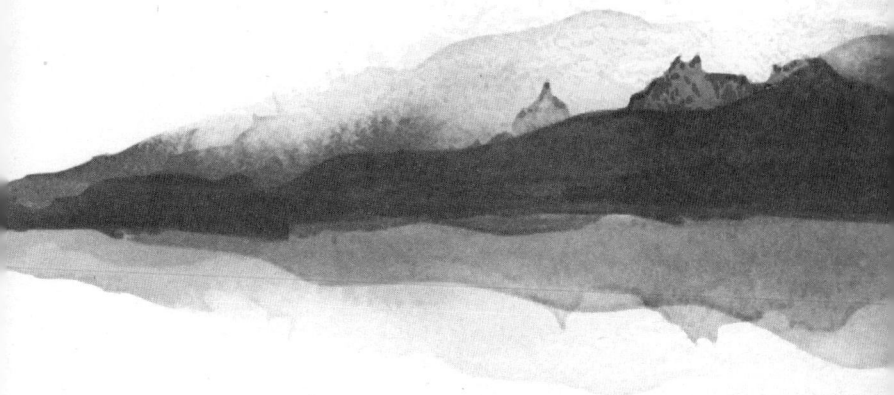

My Daughter

My daughter. I closed my eyes for one moment.
And suddenly a woman stood where my little girl used to be.
I may not be able to hold you now in my arms.
But I will always hold you close in my heart.
You have given me countless reasons to be proud of the
woman you have become.
But the proudest moment for me is telling others.
That you are my daughter.
> *I love you today, tomorrow. And always.*

Which would be worse?
To live a life filled with regrets, or to face
the unknown with the scars of experience
etched upon your soul?

#deepthoughts

Indelible Marks

No love, however brief, is wasted,
for even the fleeting moments of affection leave traces of
warmth in our hearts.
They remind us of our capacity to feel and connect.
In the mosaic of our lives, every encounter leaves, an
indelible mark.
Shaping us into,

    "Who
        we are
           meant to be."

In another place, another time . . .
We'd be better together.

#deepthoughts

I Have Found Myself

Sometimes in the dark of night I ponder
If you ever think of me and sigh
Not that I wish to have you ponder
But that I wonder if you valued my tie

But I know, that it is futile to wonder
If you ever miss me or regret
For you have moved on to another
And you have left me to forget

But I also know that I'm stronger
Than the demons in my head
For I have learned to live without you

I have found myself instead

#foundmyself

Sometimes you find forever in a kiss,
a timeless moment that lingers on the lips
and in the heart, an eternal spark that
ignites a love story for all of eternity.

#deepthoughts

The Glow of the Moon and Stars

The glow of the moon and stars above
Is nothing to the radiance of your eyes
The warmth of the sun that fills the sky
Is nothing to the tenderness of your love

The glow of the moon and stars at night
Is nothing to the brilliance of your mind
The warmth of the sun that makes life bright
Is nothing to the kindness of your mind

The glow of the moon and stars so fair
Is nothing to the beauty of your face
The warmth of the sun that fills the air
Is nothing to the comfort of your embrace

The glow of the moon and stars, the sun
Is nothing to the wonder of the one

To die is to rest, but to live is to love.

If you only listen with your ears,
I can't get in; it's through the heart and
the soul that whispers of truth and
understanding can find their way . . .
create a connection that transcends
mere words.

#deepthoughts

The Same Hand That Holds Your Hand

The same hand that holds your hand
Is the one that writes these lines
The words that flow from very my pen
Are inspired by your eyes, your soul, your smile.

You are the muse of my poetry
The reason for my rhyme
The melody of my song
The rhythm of my time

You fill my life with beauty
And make my dreams come true
You are the best thing that's ever happened to me

    My Darling

      Truly

        I love you.

Let this one sink in . . .
"There's a difference between being happy . . .
and being distracted from happiness"

#deepthoughts

Fighting for happiness?
or just settling for a distraction . . .

Versions of Love

There are many versions of love
That we can experience in life
Some are fleeting and some are lasting
Some are gentle and some are strife

There is the love of a parent
Who nurtures and protects their child
There is the love of a friend
Who supports and makes us smile

There is the love of a partner
Who shares our joys and sorrows
There is the love of a soulmate
Who connects with us on deeper levels

There is the love of a pet
Who gives us unconditional affection
There is the love of a hobby
That fills us with passion and direction

There is the love of a cause
That inspires us to make a difference
There is the love of a god
Who guides us with faith and reverence

There are many versions of love
That we can encounter in our journey
But the most important one of all
Is the love of ourselves, that of which . . .

can set us free.

"To love is to risk,
    to risk is to fear,
        to fear is to hide,
            to hide is to lose."

If you let your fear take over, you might hide your true feelings and avoid being vulnerable. But by doing so, you also lose the opportunity to experience the joy and intimacy of love. You should not let fear stop you from loving, because love is worth the risk.

"Love bravely, or lose yourself in fear."

And we ask ourselves this question:
Who got you through this year?

#deepthoughts

In My Dreams . . .

I still feel the gentle brush of your hair upon my face,
as I place my lips upon yours
the fulness of your lips
the gentle wet whisper of a million magic
moments in a lifetime of –

L
O
V
E

in my dreams . . .
you are still, my home
my stillness
my butterfly breaths

I miss you,
see you again tonight my love.

#DreamWorld

Dictionary definition:

love

noun
1.

an intense feeling of deep <u>affection</u>.

In my twenties I met the love of my life but like most young love we often don't see the honesty and purity in it. It is an unblemished love, without reserve, open and true. I believe our first love is our truest experience of a deep feeling of true unreserved affection for another soul . . . because innocent hearts are – open.

To My Children

To my children. Never forget, I love you.
I hope you believe in yourself as much as I believe in you.
When life try's to knock you down,
I will always have your back.
I can't promise to be here for the rest of your life,
but what I can promise,
is to love you for the rest of mine.

we are not perfect
we make mistakes
we hurt each other
we say sorry
we forgive
we learn
we grow
we are human
we are love

You Are My

True love is a beacon that withstands life's storms, for it knows no bounds.
You are my solace in the chaos, my calm in the midst of turmoil.
You are my laughter in moments of joy, my shoulder to lean on when tears fall.
You are my strength when I am weak, my courage when I face the unknown.
You are my sunshine on the darkest days, my guiding star through the night.
You are my home, the place where my heart finds belonging.

I love you with every breath I take.

When I stop and stare in the mirror and realise,
I'm still looking for happiness . . .
. . . in the very place I lost it.

#deepthoughts

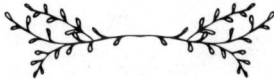

Love Me as I Am

You are the sun that lights my day
The moon that guides my night
The stars that fill my sky with grace
You are the light of my life

I don't need you to make me whole
I need you to share my soul
To challenge me, inspire me
             To support me,
                    love me as I am

You can forget someone that broke your heart . . .
But you can never forget the person who
gathered the pieces, healed your soul,
and made you smile again.
I can't thank you enough for being that person.

#deepthoughts

You know it's weird . . .
I played our slow set tonight . . .
my heart raced
and then it sat still . . .
and I don't how to feel . . .

#deepthoughts

Your presence lingers in the quiet moments of my
day, and in the restless moment of my nights.
Because you'll always be . . .
the last thought on my mind before I sleep . . .
like every night.

#deepthoughts

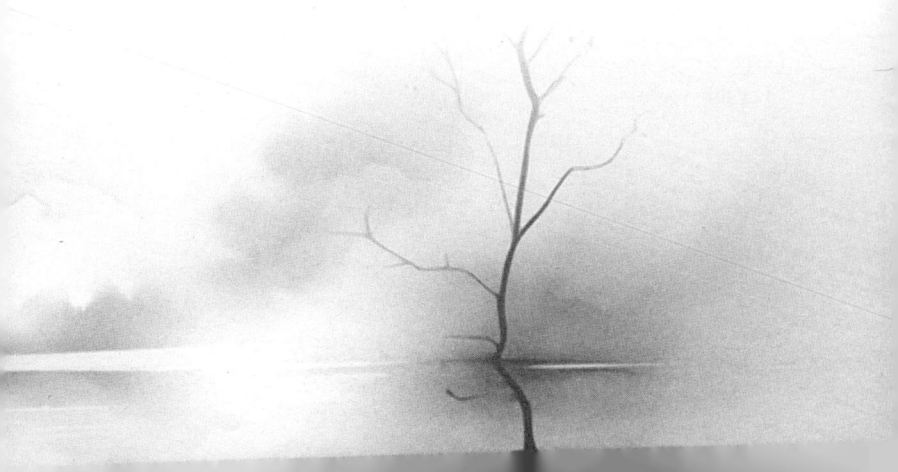

And Damn, You Were Perfect

We danced in the rain,
> and it wasn't some Hollywood moment, all clean
> and perfect. It was messy, raw, and real. The sky
> opened up, pouring down like it was trying to
> wash away all the bullshit we'd been carrying. We
> didn't care. We laughed, we shouted, we felt alive.

Love, it's . . . not the shit they sell you in those glossy
magazines. It's gritty, it's painful, it's beautiful in its own
screwed-up way. It's the way you looked at me, soaked to
the bone, hair plastered to your face, mascara running.
And damn, **you were perfect**.

We danced in the rain,
> and it was like the world finally made sense. No
> pretences, no masks. Just us, raw and exposed.
> Your hands on my shoulders, mine on your waist,
> the cold seeping through our clothes but the
> heat between us burning bright. That's Love. It's
> not neat. It's chaotic, like the storm we found
> ourselves in.

Love is standing there, drenched, shivering, and laughing
because we've got each other. It's the way you smiled
through the rain, your eyes saying everything words
couldn't. It's the way we clung to each other, finding
warmth in the middle of a downpour. Love is real, messy,
and perfectly imperfect.

We danced in the rain,
and in that moment, nothing else mattered. It was just us, two souls tangled together, fighting against the storm. That's the true feeling of love. Not some fairy tale, but two people finding a bit of magic . . . in the madness.

"It's the way you looked at me, soaked to the bone, hair plastered to your face, mascara running. And damn, you were perfect."

Some Days

Some days are filled with tears
and I don't give a damn about anything
I just sit in my room and drink
and smoke and write
and curse the world and God
and fate and you

Some days are filled with fears
and I don't have the guts to face them
I just hide in my bed and sleep
and dream and cry
and hate myself and life
and hope and you

Some days are filled with pain
and I don't have the will to fight it
I just lie on the floor and bleed
and moan and writhe
and wish for death and peace
and love and you

But you are gone
and I am alone
and nothing matters anymore
and some days are filled with nothing
but tears and fears and pain
and you
*You left me with nothing but tears,
fears, pain, and a bottle . . .*

We've not got much but we've got love to pay the bills. And that's what matters most, because love is the only currency that never loses its value.

#deepthoughts

5

nature & spirituality

If this was the last day of your life, what
would you do to make things right?
Would you say sorry to those you hurt, or
thank you to those who helped?
Would you forgive yourself for your mistakes,
or celebrate your achievements?
Would you express your love to those who
matter, or let go of those who don't?
Would you live in the present, or dwell
in the past?
Would you make peace with your fate,
or fight for your future?
The choice is yours, but remember this:
Every day could be your last, so make
every day right.

#deepthoughts

Sometimes the Stars Make Me Cry and I Don't Know Why . . .

Maybe it's because they remind me of the things I left behind

The dreams I had, the hopes I lost, the love I never found

Or maybe it's because they show me how small I am in this vast universe How insignificant my problems are, how fleeting my life is

Or maybe it's because they shine so bright, so beautiful, so pure And I feel so dark, so ugly, so flawed Or maybe it's because they are so far away, so unreachable, so distant And I long for something closer, something warmer, something real

Or maybe it's because they are so many, so diverse, so unique And I feel so lonely, so boring, so ordinary Or maybe it's because they are so silent, so peaceful, so serene And I hear so much noise, so much chaos, so much pain

Or maybe it's because they are so mysterious, so intriguing, so enchanting And I know so little, so mundane, so dull Or maybe it's because they are so different, so alien, so unknown And I fear so much, so often, so deeply

Or maybe it's because they are so constant, so faithful,
so loyal And I change so much, so easily, so quickly
Or maybe it's because they are so ancient, so wise, so
timeless And I am so young, so foolish, so mortal

Or maybe it's because they are so amazing, so wonderful,
so inspiring And I am so grateful, so humbled, so moved
Or maybe it's because they are so much more than I can
ever be And I am so much less than I can ever see

Or maybe it's because they are the stars and I am just me
And I don't know why they make me cry But I know they
make me feel alive.

Sometimes, the happiest ending isn't about finding the fairy tale we once dreamed of. It's about bravely embracing change, letting go of what no longer services us. And discovering that the true joy lies in the courage to move on . . .

#deepthoughts

The Dreamers

"I wish I wasn't such a dreamer," *she sighed*,
I am lost in the realms where fantasy resides.
In starlit visions, where reality suspends,
Imagination dances, and time, oh . . . how it transcends.

Yet, in dreaming, a world of wonders unfolds,
And in twisting dances of hope, where destinies are foretold.
For in the heart a dreamer courage can take flight,
Turning . . . wishes in to stars, that light the dark night.

And he said

"But dreamer, your wishes paint the sky,
A delectable wonder where aspirations fly.
And In the realm of dreams, I find my way,
Chasing the echoes of, come what may.

Your heart's whispers, like a gentle stream,
Please guide me through the vastness of your dream.
And as we dance the dance, in this cosmic ballet,
For your dreams and mine, together, shall sway."

> *"We are dreamers*
> *Our hearts whisper to the stars*
> *We dance in the sky"*

When the Day is Truly Done

Which way does the wind blow when the day is done,
Whispering secrets with the sinking sun?
Through fields of gold or mountains grand,
Carrying tales of times in a far-off land.

Does it dance with the leaves in a twilight waltz,
Or drift through the canyons where silence exalts?
In the echoes of dusk, its mysteries unfold,
A serenade to the night, a story yet untold.

Does it carry the fragrance of blossoms in bloom,
Or sweep through the city, where the shadows loom?
In its breath, a lullaby for the sweet weary soul,
A melody that weaves through time, making us whole.

Which way does the wind blow, in the hush of eve,
Whisking away the cares that our hearts often grieve?
In the painting of twilight, a song is spun,

Answered only . . .

when the day is truly done.

"The wind whispers secrets to the night."

Thank you, life . . .
for the kaleidoscope of experiences that have
moulded me into who I am today.
Through the endless depths of pain and the
soaring heights of love, the bitter taste of loss
and the sweet memories of connection . . .
I have learned, grown, and evolved.
Every encounter, both uplifting and
challenging, has left its mark upon my soul,
etching a story that is uniquely mine.
As I stand before my reflection and gaze into
the portals of my very being,
*"I ponder: What greater gift is there than a
life lived fully, rich with all its intricacies and
the wisdom it bestows?"*

#deepthoughts

I Was a Lost Child Too

She was a lost child
She didn't know where she belonged
She didn't know who she was
She didn't know what she wanted

She wandered from place to place
She tried different things
She met different people
She never stayed long

She was a lost child
But I loved her anyway
And I loved her wildness
I loved her freedom
I loved her unpredictability

She was a lost child
But she made me feel alive
And she made me feel something
She made me feel anything . . .

She was a lost child
And you wouldn't want me any other way
You wouldn't want me to be normal
You wouldn't want me to be boring
You wouldn't want me to be stable

You loved me because I loved her
You loved me because I was like her
You loved me because

I was a lost child too . . .

6

RESILIENCE & hope

Everyone is here to teach you something,
Some true loving them . . .
And others,
Through losing them.

#deepthoughts

Hope Flickers Patiently

Fear may loom within the shadows, but remember that darkness, in all its forms, is not eternal. Even the longest and most treacherous nights eventually surrender to the embrace of dawn, unveiling the radiant light of a new day. So trust in the cycle of life's seasons, for amidst the darkest moments, *hope flickers patiently*, awaiting its turn to illuminate your path once more.

So, hold steadfast to the unwavering belief that the light will return and cast away the shadows . . .

#hopeflickerspatiently

Hurting yourself is easy, living is hard.

#deepthoughts

Please remember that you are valuable and worthy of respect. You have the potential to overcome your challenges and achieve your goals. You have the power to change your life for the better. Hurting yourself is easy, living is hard, but you can do it. I believe in you.

I never really wanted a perfect life . . .
Just one that's happy.

#deepthoughts

I'm OK

I'm OK, ya know
>   I don't need your pity or your sympathy
>   I don't need your advice or your empathy
>   I don't need your hugs or your kisses
>   I don't need your lies or your promises

I'm OK, ya know
>   I can handle this pain and this sorrow
>   I can face this challenge and this tomorrow
>   I can heal this wound and this scar
>   I can find peace, in this wound and this scar

I'm OK, ya know
>   I have my strength and my courage
>   I have my faith and my purpose
>   I have my dreams and my goals
>   I have myself and my soul

I'm OK, ya know,
>   but sometimes . . .
>   I wish you were still here with me.

"I don't need you to make me whole"
#torn

I Have Cried All My Tears

I have cried all my tears
All that is left is anger
Anger at the world and myself
Anger at the pain and the loss

I have no more tears to shed
Only flames to burn
Burn everything that reminds me of you
Burn everything that's hurt me too

I have no more sorrow to feel
Rage, only rage to unleash
Rage at the injustice and the fate
Rage at the emptiness and the hate

I have cried all my tears
All that is left is anger
But anger is not the answer
Anger is not the healer

I need to find a way to cope
A way to heal and hope
A way to forgive and move on
A way to live and love again

#angercanconsume

The stars above whisper tales of dreams
that soared and dreams that fell.
And for a moment, I lived in all the glory
that those dreams were . . .
But . . .
There are dreams that are . . .
and dreams that aren't . . .
And I'm still coming to terms with that . . .

#deepthoughts

Most men live lives of quiet desperation,
imprisoned by the walls of isolation. I don't
know if you've ever experienced genuine
loneliness, to be consumed by the shadows of
your own mind, it leaves your heart confined.

The silence, battling inner storms, unheard.
The weight of true emptiness is suffocating.

Beneath the surface the tears silently flow,
and the world moves on.

Their smiles a facade, hiding the pain, and a
cry for help just seems brutally in vain.

I was one of those men . . . and I am not alone.

Most men live lives of quiet desperation.

#deepthoughts

Let this one sink in . . .
"Some days it takes a lot of work just to be OK.
And that's OK."

#deepthoughts

Pillows Stained with Tears

Pillows stained with tears, a silent witness to my pain, Each
drop a testament to the storms within, the falling rain.
In solitude, I weep and pour my sorrows out at night, As
darkness blankets all, and stars shed their gentle light.

Soft and yielding, these pillows cradle my despair,
Absorbing all the heartache, the burdens that I bear.
They're soaked in every drop of grief, each silent cry-,
As I wrestle with the demons that beneath my surface lie.

Through troubled dreams and restless hours, they're
there to hold, A haven for my wounded soul, in secrets
left untold. They keep my fragile heart afloat in the ocean
of my fears, These pillows stained with tears, they've
witnessed countless years.

But those pillows bear the truth of pain upon their very
case. A testament to battles fought within the dead of night.

Pillows stained with tears
               . . . my silent fight.

Sunday anxiety can be overwhelming.
But it's important to remember that a new
week is an opportunity to start fresh and
tackle the any challenges with positivity
and determination.
Embrace each day with an open mind.
And the belief in yourself to make it a
great one.

#deepthoughts

The journey towards healing is not always
a straight path.
It's a winding road and sometimes it's
a lonely one.
But you have to keep walking.
Because eventually, the pain will fade,
And the sun will rise again.

#deepthoughts

There comes a time in life when you realise that all of the hurt, heartbreak and pain you've experienced in your lifetime has granted you with the wisdom to face the world, in a way you never thought possible. In order to love the person you are, you cannot hate the experiences that shaped you.

#deepthoughts

A Life Without Dreams

There goes that dream, that once was mine to keep
The dream of love, of happiness, of peace
The dream that made me smile, that made me weep
The dream that filled my heart, that gave me ease

But now that dream is gone, it's slipped away
The dream of love, of happiness, of peace
The dream that turned to dust, that turned to grey
The dream that broke my heart, that gave me grief

And yet that dream still lingers, in my mind
The dream of love, of happiness, of peace
The dream that haunts me, that I can't unwind
The dream that stirs my soul, that won't release

There goes that dream, that once was mine to keep
But still that dream remains, without it, I cannot sleep

"Life without dreams

Is like a sky without stars

Empty and silent"

#dreamers

I am, lost in the dark, but I don't give up on hope I know there's a light that can carry me home I just have to find it, or let it find me I'm lost in the dark but I'm not alone

#deepthoughts

The Words We Crave

Why do we crave the poems that speak our fears?
The ones that voice the secrets of our hearts
The ones that show the pain behind our scars
The ones that make us shed our bitter tears

Why do we love the poems that spark our hopes?
The ones that inspire us to change and grow
The ones that challenge us to learn and know
The ones that help us understand and cope

Why do we need the poems that share our dreams?
The ones that express our deepest desires
The ones that ignite our creative fires
The ones that connect us with life's extremes

Perhaps we seek the poems that make us feel
The ones that show us what is true and is real . . .

Perhaps, people want to read poems
with the words they're afraid to say . . .

"You can't change your past, but you change your perspective."
By shifting our perspective, we can change the impact our past has had on our present and future. Including things like learning from past mistakes, finding the positive in negative experiences and letting go of regrets and or resentment.
Changing our perspective can help us move forward in a more positive and productive way.

#deepthoughts

You Are Not Alone

You may feel like you are trapped in a dark hole
With no way out and no one to console
You may think that you have no reason to live
That you have nothing to offer and nothing to give

But you are not alone in this fight
There are people who care and want to help you see the light
There are resources and services that can guide you through
There are stories of survival that can inspire you too.

You are not alone in this pain
There are others who have been there and have overcome the same
There are possibilities and opportunities that await you
There are dreams and goals that you can pursue

You are not alone in this world
You are a beautiful and wonderful human being with a destiny

So please don't give up on yourself or your life
Please reach out for help and don't be afraid to ask
Please remember that you are not alone and that you matter
Please know that you are strong and that you can recover

#hopeisthelight

"Hope is what keeps us moving forward"

It's never too late . . .

#deepthoughts

AUTHOR'S NOTE

In the end, life is a precious gift that we must cherish and make the most of. And to requote the poem "The Dash" it reminds us, what truly matters is not the dates on our tombstone, but the dash in between, which represents the life we lived, the love we shared, and the impact we made.

Therefore, let us not take life for granted, but rather embrace it with all its joys and sorrows, its triumphs and failures, its beauty and complexity. Let us seek truth, wisdom, and compassion, and share them with others, knowing that we are all in this together.

I want to express my heartfelt gratitude and love to all who read these words, and to all who have touched my life in one way or another. May we continue to learn, grow, and inspire each other, and may our lives be filled with joy, peace, and purpose.

Thank you, and God bless.

Jamie

ACKNOWLEDGEMENTS

First and foremost, a big thank you to my family. Without your constant reminders that "poetry doesn't pay the bills", I might have pursued a sensible career . . . oh wait I did too, win? Your unwavering support (and occasional eyerolls) have shaped me into the poet I am. And to the uniquely beautiful moments we've had in life – which more importantly have shaped me into the person I am today – along with your love, laughter and the tears we've shared. Some say I'm alright and some not, but you know what, feck them.

Social media has given a new perspective on the life I've lived. I know not all of you have shared the same experience in life and for that I am truly sorry. But I'm a firm believer in writing your own story. I hope you have the courage to make the changes to rewrite your story and give it a happy ending.

> "It's never too late to be what you might have been."

To my friends, who have endured countless late-night readings and pretentious ~~coffee shop~~ drunken discussions. Your friendship means the world to me, even if you still don't understand half of what I write. Special shoutout to those who pretended to read my drafts – your acting skills deserve an Oscar.

Individual Shoutouts:

Kristen – For always being the first to say, "This is great!" even when it clearly wasn't. Your optimism is both baffling and appreciated. Kristen "It needs more emotion Jamie . . . emotion".

Mason – For your endless supply of sarcastic comments (woke Canadian life has changed you). You kept me awake and humble but you'll always be just a Northsider to me.

Bilco – For pretending to understand my metaphors. Your nodding and thoughtful expressions were very convincing. Maybe we should just stick to the drinking together, pal? Survivors lad – Morty.

Dean – For your brutal honesty. Your feedback was harsh but necessary (on my gaming skills mostly). I owe you a drink (or ten). "Helllooo Jackie."

Audrey – For always being there to remind me that "real jobs" exist. Your practicality kept me grounded, sort of . . . with fear alone. Special shout out to Craig, no pun intended.

My sisters – Madalyn and Leonie . . . you're both amazing women and I love you dearly but it's time to let the cat out of the bag. I've always told you individually that "you're my favourite sister" – I'll say no more!

My brother – Marcus for all the times we slapped each other's heads and all the laughs. I'm so proud of the man you are today, we all are. And I know Mam would have been especially proud of you.

My parents – Pauline and James Mooney. I grew up in the dream home. Full of love and excitement, with all the truly amazing values that embody a loving family. Possibly the wealthiest family I know . . . not financially, but in heart, soul and happiness. I just can't thank you enough.

I was going to share some of my moments, but I think I'll keep them for me. But I will leave you with this simple line from a letter from my mother, "*I love you, I'm proud of you, love Mammy*". And its still something I take out from time to time, just to you know . . . see the words again.

One from Dad. Midway through recruit training, I didn't think I'd make it. I had my weekly call from the public phone box in the naval base and he answered. I told him I was going to quit. The following has lived with me all my life: "*You can't, you're my son, you show those (insert derogatory word for country folk) what the Dubs can do, it's just a moment of weakness and that'll pass and tomorrow will be a new day. Plus, we've already booked the hotel for your passing out and it's non-refundable!*"

His advice has always been empowering, supportive and delivered with a little humour. I've taken the same approach with my own kids.

Speaking of which, to my daughter, Caoimhe, and sons, Ben and Warren. I am so proud of you all. I love you with all my heart. You give me the energy to live.

Finally, a special shoutout to Kristen Taylor.

> "Sometimes it takes a great woman to show a man he can be more than he thought he could be."

My best friend and the finest believer in my poetic prowess. Without you, I'd still be rhyming "cat" with "hat" and thinking it was pure genius. Your support has been like a pint of the finest alcohol on a rainy day – essential and wonderfully uplifting, just like you.

#3amdances #hitthedif

Here's to you, Kristen, for proving that behind every great poet is an even greater friend who knows when to hand over the pen and when to hand over the beverraginos.

And last but not least . . . to you, the person holding this book. You have enabled a dream for me, I am truly thankful. To all of you that have followed me, supported, shared and commented on my posts. You gave me the confidence to be bigger than I thought possible.

I love you.

And finally, to everyone who said, "You should write a book!" – well, here it is.

I hope you're happy now.

I did it . . .

The Wandering Paddy, aka James Mooney,
is an Irish author and voiceover artist from Dublin.
After a career in the military, he now has a successful
career in IT as well as working on his poetry and writing.
Jamie is a cancer survivor, an experience which has had
a major impact on his work. His social media following
is growing rapidly and is now approaching 600,000
followers across all channels.

@the.wanderingpaddy on Instagram
@thewanderingpaddy on TikTok
@TheWanderingPaddy on Facebook